A Rose From Heaven

D1518113

A Rose From Heaven

A Memoir

Lauren Maria Vignola

The events and conversations in this book have been set down to the best of the author's ability, although some names and details have been changed to protect the privacy of individuals.

Copyright © 2024 by Lauren M. Vignola

All rights reserved. No part of this book may be reproduced or used in any manner without written permission of the copyright owner except for the use of quotations in a book review. For more information, address: midvig19@verizon.net.

First paperback edition January 2024

Cover Photography by Gemini Pro Studio

Book Cover Stock File ID: 1317730252

ISBN: 9798873899463 (paperback)

DEDICATION

To Mother Mary for praying to God for

me; and to my parents for always being

there for me.

My Message

I am an epitome of God's greatest gift, life. It is my belief when God gives us a blessing it is not meant for oneself but to share with everyone. After having survived two intense brain tumors, and with limited eyesight and mobile capability, I have spent the past five years writing with a one-handed keyboard and a computer that audibly reports back to me what I'm doing. This is my story and I believe it should be shared.

~

ACKNOWLEDGEMENTS

I want to express special thanks to God, Mother Mary, and all of the people around the world that prayed for me through the years as well as when I was diagnosed with a brain tumor when I was a baby.

- ❖ Thanks to my parents, Maria and Carmine, for your unconditional love and never ending support.

- ❖ To my sister, Mary-Christine, for always being there for me through thick and thin.

- ❖ To my brothers, David and Carmine, for never treating me any differently.

- ❖ To Ryan and Marcy, for your constant encouragement.

- ❖ To Bettie, for being a wonderful friend and

supporting me.

- ❖ To Lori, thank you for being a remarkable part of my life.

- ❖ Special thank you to the teachers and staff at New Life Christian School who sparked my passion for writing.

- ❖ I am extremely grateful to Laura for her love and patience in spending countless evenings helping me edit and publish this book.

- ❖ To my grandparents for their love and also my aunts and uncles for their encouragement and for always letting me know they care when traveling to visit me when I was in the hospital and at home.

- ❖ A special thanks to Rachael and Anthony LoRusso who adopted me as their granddaughter and prayed for me unceasingly.

- ❖ Although he is in heaven now I want to thank a very special man, Father Denis Kelleher and his healing ministry for making sure my family and I traveled with them on many pilgrimages and for their constant prayers.

- ❖ A heartfelt thanks to all the priests and sisters who have prayed for me in the past and continue to pray for me.

- ❖ A special thank you to Joseph Sperrazza who helped my parents during our darkest times.

- ❖ To all my nieces and nephews, thank you for keeping me entertained and showering me with your love and companionship. I love

you all very much.

CONTENTS

~

Life is precious so don't take anything

for granted.

~

CHAPTER ONE

The Queen of Brooklyn and The King of Queens

Jesus answered, "Haven't you read the scripture
that says that in the beginning the Creator made
people male and female? And God said, "For this
reason a man will leave his father and mother and
unite with his wife, and the two will become one. So
they are no longer two, but one. Man must not
separate, then, what God has joined together."

- Matthew 19:4-6

I came into this world the same way we all did. I was the third of my parents' four children. My siblings and I were born into a tight-knit Italian family. But in order for you to know my story, I must begin by telling you my parents' story. My parents are New Yorkers, my mom being a queen of Brooklyn and my father a king of Queens.

Let's begin with our queen of Brooklyn. In 1979, the night began with three friends going to a dance on Long Island, a forty-five minute drive from Brooklyn. This is when it got interesting, the queen, Maria, and her friends got a flat tire on the way to the dance. When they tried to fix the flat and were filthy from the road, an older gentleman came to their rescue. He asked them if they needed help changing the tire and the girls said, "Yes."

After the gentleman fixed the tire, the queen was exhausted and wanted to go home. However, her friends insisted that they still go out and dance. Maria was persuaded to go out to a local disco in Brooklyn which was closer to home.

Despite the border that separates their boroughs, the king and queen's paths crossed this night at the local Brooklyn disco. Toward the end of the dance, my mom's girlfriend wanted her to meet a guy she had seen earlier in the night so she introduced this man, Carmine, to my mother. It was love at first sight but the queen approached cautiously. Unbeknownst to her at the time, he would one day become her husband.

A week after they met, Carmine went on vacation to Club Med in Martinique. On the first day he met Maria's sister, Lorraine, and her cousin Kathy. They had fun talking, and asked someone to take a group photo at the end of the night.

After the trip, my Aunt Lorraine shared her stories about her trip with my mother, and told her about the guy she met, whom she felt would be great for my mother.

A few weeks later, Lorraine showed Maria the group photo. My mom saw Carmine. "That's the same guy I met at the dance. We're actually going on a date." Some may consider this to be a coincidence, but my parents knew it was Divine Intervention.

On the eve of my parents' first date, my aunt answered the door. To Carmine's surprise, he'd already met his date's sister. Boy, was he shocked!

That got the ball rolling for them.

Five years later, they exchanged wedding vows and along the way they were blessed to have three other children besides me.

CHAPTER TWO

The Beginning of What was Expected to be the End.

"The Lord is near to those who are discouraged; he saves those who have lost all hope."

-   Psalm 34:18

When I was a baby, I was doing what a normal two-year-old would do, including walking and talking. Unfortunately, I had a setback, and I started falling down a lot. My parents took me to my regular pediatrician, and she said I was falling down a lot because of a DPT vaccine I was given a few weeks earlier. It caused me to favor my right side when I was walking. After a few weeks with no change, my parents took me to another pediatrician for a second opinion. This pediatrician had a suspicion that there was a problem with my leg either a broken bone or tumor. My parents were then referred to a neurologist who ordered scans of my leg. After the scans came back showing there was nothing, the neurologist did some further testing and referred us to another doctor at New

York University (NYU) Hospital in New York City.

When we arrived at the hospital, the doctors analyzed me by throwing a ball at me and noticed that I had a slight weakness in my arm that made me unable to react to the ball. Therefore, one of the neurologists decided to do a CT scan of my brain and discovered a large astrocytoma tumor in my brain.

This neurologist did not tell us what she had found, but referred us to another doctor at NYU Hospital. The other doctor looked over the scans and told us that I had an astrocytoma tumor going into my brain stem, from which no child has ever survived. This tumor was inoperable.

At two years old, I was too young to understand what was happening to me. NYU doctors said that they could do radiation to treat it, but that would damage everything around the tumor, including healthy brain tissue. Because the tumor was very deep in my brain, and I was so young, radiation would cause excessive brain damage.

We went to Sloan Kettering Institute to get their medical opinion on treatment options because NYU doctors said there was not much they could do. At that time, the doctors at Sloan Kettering suggested starting chemotherapy immediately which was really scary, so my parents asked the logical question: "How many children have survived this treatment with this type of tumor?". The doctors said, "No child has survived this type of tumor", so mom said no to the chemotherapy.

According to the two well-known hospitals for treating children's cancer their final decision was to make me comfortable since I had only about one year to live.

CHAPTER THREE

Hope On The Horizon

Do not be afraid--I am with you!

I am your God---let nothing terrify you!

I will make you strong and help you;

I will protect you and save you.

- *Isaiah 41:10*

Around this time I was in a Catholic nursery program. A teachers' aide at my nursery school had a friend who had an aneurysm which was treated by a doctor in Canada. Knowing about my condition, the teacher aid told my parents about this doctor. When my parents called the doctor's office at his hospital, they found out that he only dealt with aneurysms and couldn't operate on tumors, but my parents were referred by them to a doctor from Austria whose practice was now in Virginia. This Austrian doctor did a type of proton radiation therapy which uses an external beam. When my parents called the doctor he happened to be at a conference at NYU and was willing to get in touch with my doctors to get the results of my tests. After looking over my scans he didn't feel his treatment would be appropriate for my case. However, he knew of a doctor in Freiburg, Germany, Professor Fritz Mundinger who had positive results treating this type of tumor with radiation implants.

At this time, my parents did not have access to a computer so they had to go to the medical library in New York City to look up Dr. M's information. After doing the research they called the doctor and had my scans and records delivered to him in Germany. Another couple of weeks passed. Then Dr. M called saying he felt confident he would be able to help me. He explained his treatment to my parents saying he would put a radiation seed on a catheter and put it directly into the tumor. This method ensured that the radiation wouldn't go into the rest of the brain and cause unnecessary damage. When my parents had talked to the doctors at NYU about Doctor M treatment, they found out that the doctors at NYU had already known about Dr. M's treatment, but didn't tell my parents about Dr. M because they didn't think his treatment would work.

This information being withheld was a disappointment to my parents because they thought this critica information shouldn't be withheld, especially since my parents had previously asked if there was anyone in the world that could possibly help me. The doctors ultimately approved of Professor M, a world-renowned surgeon and gave us their blessing.

When I was three years old, we took a plane to Freiburg, Germany to get treatment from Dr. M.

My parents told me how amazed they were at how clean the hospitals were there. The doctor even gave my parents a room and a bed beside me. I had the procedure done and had to stay there for about a week afterwards.

After the procedure and while I was recuperating, the staff felt it was necessary for my parents to take me outside to enjoy the spring air. They provided us with a carriage and gave directions on how to go to the nearby city of Freiburg. While in town we visited the Freiburger Munster Cathedral where my parents prayed and lit candles for my recovery and healing.

When the staff at the hospital saw my parents bring me back after our visit into town, the staff immediately brought dinner to my hospital room. They kept my food warm even though we had had dinner out in town. They were very caring. Now that I'm older, I'm touched by how wonderfully they treated my family and me.

On another occasion, while I was still in the hospital the anesthesiologist invited my family to have dinner with her and her husband. Looking back, I feel astonished that she did this. It was very thoughtful of her and something that you don't often hear about American doctors doing with their patients. She told my mom and dad that she received permission from my doctor for her husband to pick us up from the hospital for dinner and he would drive us back to the hospital afterward. They made us a traditional German dinner of schnitzel and potatoes. From what I heard the food and conversation was wonderful. The family said they were very moved with emotion by the bravery of a family coming to another country, not knowing what to expect, in order to get their child the treatment she needed to save her life. My family kept in contact with this family and, in fact, they came to visit us in America several times.

After a week we went back home to the United States where I had tests done to monitor how I was doing. While recuperating I received physical, occupational and speech therapy several times a week. Medical tests were done often and each time my parents had them mailed to my doctor in Germany. At my nine month MRI scan, Dr. M said the tumor was getting smaller and it was time to remove the implant.

At first, the oncologist from the NYU team told my parents that we would have to return to Germany to get the implant removed in about eight to twelve months after it was put in, as my doctors in the U.S. wouldn't be able to do the removal procedure. Ultimately, that wasn't correct, because the head surgeon at NYU disagreed and I had the operation at NYU after all.

CHAPTER FOUR

Mother Mary and Medjugorje

A few days later Jesus went back to Capernaum, and the news spread that he was at home. So many people came together that there was no room left, not even out in front of the door. Jesus was preaching the message to them when four men arrived, carrying a paralyzed man to Jesus. Because of the crowd, however, they could not get the man to him. so they made a hole in the roof right above the place where Jesus was. When they had made an opening, they let the man down, lying on his mat. Seeing how much faith they had, Jesus said to the paralyzed man. "My son, your sins are forgiven."

- *Mark 2:1-5*

A month or two later, I started getting very weak even though I had been previously walking, talking, and generally high-functioning. I could hardly stay awake or pick my head up and was unable to sit up. My doctors ordered another scan to see why I was having these problems.

The day we went for the results of the scan, the appointment was scheduled for 11 A.M. We arrived on time but the doctors indicated they could not see us until a little after 1P.M. The team of doctors were having a tumor board meeting after which they would be able to talk to us. We were to meet with the head oncologist at 1P.M. to receive the new results. We had some time to spare so my parents decided to go to the noon mass at a little church up the street from the hospital. My father, always being the calm one, experienced a spiritual moment in the church where he could not understand so he said nothing.

As we started the meeting the oncologist said, "After the tumor board meeting we were all in agreement that the tumor was now expanding and very enlarged." The meaning of this was the end of my life and I had just a short time to live.

The doctors told my parents that they could now start me on chemotherapy to make the end of my life more comfortable. The oncologist then said that I could be put in the hospital and kept comfortable until the end.

My parents decided to take me home. My father was completely caught off guard, but my mother encouraged him not to give up as they left

the office and told the doctors we would go home
and think about it, we would not start any treatment
yet. They needed to go home and talk about this
rather than put me in the hospital room as they
continued to fight for my life. At this time, my
parents belonged to a prayer group at our local
church in Staten Island. Our friends in the prayer
group had actually just gotten back from a
pilgrimage to pray to Mother Mary in the town of
Medjugorje, a village in the municipality of Citluk,
in Bosnia-Herzegovina.

In 1981, several children were walking in
the hamlet of Bijakovici in Medjugorje, when a
woman holding an infant appeared high on a hill
among boulders and branches of Mount Podbrdo.
They immediately knew it was the Virgin Mary, but

they did not approach her. These two girls and four other children felt called to return the next day when Our Blessed Mother drew them to her. They got on their knees and began to pray. She prayed with them and promised to return the next day.

Mother Mary identified herself as the Queen of Peace, coming on a mission of Peace with a message for the world. "I have come to tell the world that God exists." Since then, Mother Mary has been appearing to them, giving them messages for the world's salvation. Each child has received individual sacred messages from Mother Mary, some were personal messages and others were for the whole world. Eventually, the children started receiving the apparitions in the choir loft at St. James Church.

My parents, being physically exhausted and emotionally crushed after their last meeting with the doctors, went home and discussed the events of that day. It was a very emotional time, as one can only imagine. There was a moment in the kitchen when my brother Carmine, who is a year older than I, heard my parents crying and, in an attempt to make them feel better, offered them a small candy valentine heart. My mother politely told him she did not want the candy but he insisted. My father, sensing how upset Carmine was, took one of the candies and on it read, "hope". My dad checked all the other candies that were in the box and not one other candy had the word "hope" on it. All the hearts in the box had either, love you, kiss me, hug me, etc. on them. My family felt this was a sign to have hope and trust in God.

At this point my father told me it was the first time in this struggle that he said to God, " I accept that my daughter is going to die, if it's your will. The only thing is that I know with her loss, I am going to die. I feel my heart breaking." Then he said to my mother, "We are going to the "Gate of Heaven" and ask if we could keep our daughter," not knowing that Mother Mary is called The Gate of Heaven. The next day, they were in contact with the people from our prayer group and started making plans to take a pilgrimage to Medjugorje with my brother and me.

We stayed in Medjugorje to pray to Mother Mary. I am extremely proud of my parents for choosing to turn to God to help me otherwise I might never have experienced the healing power of God and Mother Mary.

The atmosphere in Medjugorje is one of peace, love, and prayer. While walking to church in the morning you might see a group of people walking together praying the rosary or some teenagers sitting under a tree singing praise while someone is playing the guitar. There are also long lines of pilgrims waiting to go to confession outside of Saint James Church. It is truly heaven on earth.

At Medjugorje, after my dad carried me up Cross Mountain, we sat at the foot of the cross with his back to the wind to shield me. My mother was kneeling in prayer in front of the cross and my brother Carmine was exploring and peeling candle wax off the ground. Then a group of pilgrims from

Parma, Italy approached us. They asked if I was ill and my dad said I was. Then they asked if they could pray for me and my dad said, "Of course, I would love for you to pray for my daughter".

After they prayed they walked away then came back an hour later. The only one in the group who spoke English said that Jesus had spoken to her heart and she told my parents, "Your daughter has an illness in her brain and he wants us to pray for her". She also added , "The illness has been there since her birth". My parents told me no one knew that the illness could have been there since my birth. The doctors did tell them earlier in my diagnosis the tumor could have been there since birth because of its large size. My parents never shared that information with anyone, not even family. It is totally impossible for people from different parts of the world, the pilgrims from Parma, Italy, and us from Staten Island, New York, to meet on a mountain in what was then Yugoslavia and know so much personal information about me. Before we left the mountain, addresses were exchanged so they could correspond.

Years later, we met this group again but this time in Parma, Italy and I remember it well. We had dinner with them in a restaurant, Al Fresco, which is dining outside. There was a trellis with a long table underneath. The dinner consisted of all the specialties of that region in Italy. Before leaving, one of the group's sons, Luca, gave me a gift of perfume from Parma. I still have the perfume bottle.

When we were walking to Saint James

Church in Medjugorje one morning, saying the

rosary, my dad asked Father Allen who was

accompanying us if it would be possible for my

mother and me to get into the choir loft at the time

of the apparitions. The priest indicated it would be

impossible because of the thousands of people there

who also want to be in the choir loft. Then my

father quoted from the Bible the story of the

paralyzed man who was lowered through the roof so

he could reach Jesus. The priest was still a little bit

hesitant, but my dad said, "I would kick the door

down to get my daughter up to the choir loft if I had

to." The priest said, "Carmine, you know that you

will be arrested if you were to do that." After that

the priest promised my dad he would try but he first

had to talk to the pastor of Saint James to get his

permission.

Father Allen was able to get permission for my mother and me to go up into the choir loft. In the loft, there were visionaries, several young priests and us. We started saying the rosary and a short while later the visionaries saw The Blessed Mother. This was known through the visionaries kneeling down and immediately lifting their heads towards heaven. The experience was intense and surreal. As soon as the visionaries knelt to indicate that they saw the apparition of Mary my mom knelt along with everyone in the choir loft and the whole church. My mother extended her arms with my head on one arm and legs on another. My mother lost all the words she had prepared to say to Our Lady, so she just said, "Mother, you know why we're here."

At the time, I was on a large dose of strong steroids, so I was quite heavy for a toddler and so weak I couldn't even lift my head. However, while my mom was praying, my mom felt my head lift out of her arms just for a moment. Shortly after that, we went back downstairs to my dad and brother. My dad asked my mom if anything had happened in the choir loft. My mom told him that we had just prayed and nothing really happened. She figured that when she had felt my head lift out of her arms, it was just because of her excitement, and it hadn't actually happened, as this was such an emotional experience.

The next day, a priest named Father Joseph, approached my father and told him that he had a vision of me while he was in his room at home praying. Upon hearing this, my dad got my mom so she could hear the priest's story as well. He had a vision of Mary kissing me on the head and giving me a rose. His vision coincided with the experience my mom had when she prayed to Mother Mary. So with that, my mom told the priest that she had felt my head lift up out of her arms. My mom hadn't felt me in her arms, when I was kissed and given a rose by Mother Mary. That's when I felt the love of two mothers.

My parents along with Father Joseph met with the pastor of the church to tell him all the details of the past two days and he immediately stated, "Your daughter is healed."

Directly across the street was a small cafe. My parents ordered coffee and a hot chocolate for my brother while I was asleep in the stroller. As they were sitting there pondering the events, I suddenly woke up and told them I wanted to stand up. You can imagine the joy they felt because prior to that moment I could not stay awake and did not have the strength to stand up. My mom and dad each held one side of me, and I was able to stay up on my feet without collapsing. I stood up and walked with them. I was more alert throughout the day, as well.

Eventually, we left Medjugorje and came home to the United States where I was scheduled to have a PET scan. At the time this was a new technology using nuclear medicine. Since it was new we had to go all the way out to Long Island to get this test done. For various reasons the New York

University Hospital was unable to get the medical team to the location on Long Island to perform the PET Scan. When they finally got it together and told us to go, it was on the day of Passover, a Jewish Holy Day. I was medicated and slept in the machine that produced photos of my brain. My father saw the doctor looking at the pictures in a sense of amazement. He approached the doctor and asked him what are you seeing. The doctor replied, "This is nothing I expected to see, before coming here I reviewed her scans at NYU and I saw a very large and aggressive tumor. All I can see now is a scar on the brain. I have only one concern now and that is her vision. I want her to meet with the head of our neurological ophthalmology department. But before that I am ordering a special eye test for her using lights to check her vision." As we were left

the entire staff came outside cheering and clapping

hands as they were amazed by and ecstatic about

what they had just witnessed.

My parents then took me to a

neuro-ophthalmologist at NYU where a scan was

performed. When we saw the ophthalmologist he

examined me and told them, "Your daughter is

completely blind." My father asked the doctor if I

could see anything and the doctor responded, "No,

she doesn't even see light." The ophthalmologist

said that there was no way that I would ever get my

vision back.

Throughout my illness, my parents had

taken me to many healing masses including one in

Worcester, Massachusetts, a Catholic Mass by

Father Ralph D'Orio. When hearing I was blind, my mother was heartbroken and told my father, "Lauren has always been afraid of the dark and now she's in darkness." My father's response was, "She will see again." A few days later we drove approximately 405 miles to attend one of Father DiOrio healing masses.

CHAPTER FIVE

Hidden Blessings

"O Lord, you give me light;

you dispel my darkness."

-    *Psalm 18:28*

The service was much longer than a usual mass and at one point my brother became restless. My mom walked out of the room with him. While she was in the next room she heard my dad on the loudspeaker saying that his daughter saw light, and my mom rushed back into the room. My mom was very skeptical. She thought that my dad wanted to believe something that hadn't happened, just because he had wanted it so badly. As my father tells me, he almost didn't go up to claim my healing because he remembered the doctor telling him, "She'll never see again, it's impossible." Then he remembered what the Angel Gabriel told Mary when she questioned how she could have a child, since she had no relation with a man, and the Angel said, "There is nothing God cannot do."

My mother tested me when we went home by sticking her tongue out, and I did the same right back to her, so she realized that my dad had been telling the truth. We then went back to my neuro-ophthalmologist who had previously said that I was completely blind and couldn't even see light. He was stunned and said, "I cannot believe this, there is no medical term to describe it." My father asked the doctor if he would consider this a miracle and the doctor said, "Yes, this is a miracle."

After receiving the gift of sight, a prayer group friend of my parents called and wanted my mother to go to Medjugorje to pray with her. This woman's daughter, who was in her mid 20's, was supposed to go with her mother but she had cancer and wasn't doing well enough to travel. My mother thanked her but told her we just returned from Medjugorje and asked her to offer the trip to someone else. About a week later, the woman called back and said she could not find anyone to take this trip, so she asked my mother to reconsider. My parents talked and prayed about it then decided that if there was another seat available on the plane for me, we would go. Shortly after that the agency called and said there was only one extra seat on the plane available. My parents took that as a sign from Mother Mary for me and my mother to go to Medjugorje once again.

Although we went on this trip with the prayer group there were many times my mother found herself isolated and alone. One day, when my mother was by herself, she was trying to climb

Cross Mountain holding me in her arms. She got to a point when she felt she could no longer take another step so she decided to sit on the rocks and pray. Her prayer was asking God to help her get to the top of the mountain. Within minutes a woman, large in stature, just picked me up from my mothers arms and carried me to the top of the mountain. This woman never said a word and when they got to the top just placed me back in my mother's arms. My mother never saw her again. Another blessed moment which happened was many people in the prayer group were very skeptical that I had vision because my eyelids were mostly closed as another result of the brain tumor. One night after dinner my mother took out a Winnie the Pooh stuffed animal along with other items and when she held them up in front of me, she asked me to identify each object which I did without a problem. The people in our group were ecstatic and no longer questioned my ability to see.

CHAPTER SIX

My Education

"Watch yourself and watch your teaching.

Keep on doing these things, because if you

do, you will save both yourself and those who

hear you."

- *1 Timothy 4:16*

I had made normal progress early in life, including lifting my head, crawling, walking and speaking. Unfortunately, all my progress was destroyed by the tumor, so I had to relearn everything.

Throughout my youth, I was able to navigate school without a problem. I was able to walk but with a limp because my right leg is longer than my left leg. I had a lisp and struggled with articulation therefore I went to speech therapy when I was younger. Unfortunately I've required aides all my life, however, I still worked hard and received good grades as the aides were only there to help take notes.

When I was growing up, the teachers where we lived at that time told my parents that I couldn't learn. When I started school, I was placed in a low functioning class where there was hardly any learning and most of the day was playing with toys. They didn't want to teach me because even though the tumor was gone, it had left me with a left side weakness, low vision and a speech problem.

At the time I started Kindergarten in 1990 most schools were not open to inclusion or accommodating students with special needs, so my parents, along with specialists in education, found a school in upstate New York where they had just started an inclusion program. I was thriving in school until I reached fifth grade and was getting ready to enter middle school. We found out that the school had been given a grant for their inclusion program and the grant was ending. They no longer wanted to make accommodations for me and school was becoming stressful for me. Beside school problems my parents were not content with living upstate. The winters were long and cold and my father, even though retired, wanted to get a job which was difficult since we lived in a very small town. We again started to look around for a place to accommodate my needs and my family's. That is when we moved to Maryland where I finally found a school that I felt wanted me. The school made the accommodations I needed, which was large print material, a scribe who was an aide. When I ask my parents, "Do you have any regrets moving down here for me?", they reply, "No, because our children come first." In addition, my father was able to find a job as a teacher in public school.

All was going well until high school, when again everything I needed to achieve success seemed to be a problem. One example was that the occupational therapist told me I would never be able to write my name. Another was asking the school to provide a one-handed keyboard, since I only had use of my right hand. My parents went to many meetings throughout my middle and high school years.

In high school, one of the meetings was because I tripped in the hallway. The students wanted to help me up but my aide wanted them to leave me on the ground. The aide said, "You would pull her arm out of her socket." So the aide left me on the ground for all to see. The teachers helped me get back up. I was so humiliated when the bus dropped me off. I was crying from the embarrassment of this traumatic event.

When I told my parents about the incident, they were furious. They went down to the school to have a talk with the principal. No one wanted to be held accountable for what had happened.

Another experience I had was when my aide didn't let me participate in CPR. She thought "something was going to happen ". To this day we don't know what she meant. Another one of many incidents that stands out for me is when my parents were told I couldn't learn algebra. They failed to mention that I had been taken out of my class and put in the hallway to be taught by my aide who herself had no knowledge of algebra.

My parents took me out of school then

because there was no reasoning with the teachers or administration. It was clear they were not capable of teaching a person with any type of special needs and unwilling to make accommodations. My parents were looking into some private schools and filled out some applications. We had a meeting with one of the nearby Christian Schools but when we didn't hear back, my parents decided to homeschool. We received all the books for homeschooling when the Christian School called and requested another interview. When we arrived there, the principal, staff and teachers said, "We would love it if you'd come to our school but we don't have the funds to hire an aide for her."

So, my saintly mom quit her job for me and worked as my aide without pay. After a while I didn't need her to sit in my classes with me because my classmates would take notes for me. She would only help me in math class because I needed help writing my solutions out on paper. I used to walk around the grounds with my mother in between classes. It was very beautiful. The school had a lovely lake and horses on the other side of the building. I took Rhythmic Writing because I didn't know how to write in cursive, which is something one of my favorite teachers taught me to do. My other favorites were my math teacher and my history teacher, even though she thought I said a bad word one time when I had only said "shucks." She sent me to the principal's office. Thankfully, he believed me when I told him that's not what I said because I hadn't ever spoken that way before.

I graduated with honors, and I was on the Dean's List. When I walked across the stage to receive my diploma, I received a standing ovation. I was blessed to have my whole family at the graduation, especially my grandparents. After the graduation ceremony my classmates and I threw our hats up in the air, and then we received gifts from our vice principal. I received a photo flip album and a painted rock with the name of my school on it along with Joshua 4:20-24. This verse says: There Joshua set up the twelve stones taken from the Jordan. And he said to the people of Israel, "In the future, when your children ask you what these stones mean, you will tell them that the Lord your God dried up the water of the Jordan for you until you had crossed, just as he dried up the Red

Sea for us. Because of this everyone on earth will know how great the Lord's power is, and you will honor the Lord your God forever." I still have the rock in my garden in front of Mother Mary's Statue. I graduated in 2005, fortunately, through the grace of God, my parents found an accessible Christian school. To this day, I am grateful that we found it.

After high school, I enrolled in courses at Frederick Community College where I took two courses at a time to pace myself with the college workload. In the time I was there I took Human Growth and Development, Social Studies, Death and Dying, and Writing. The school made accommodations for me. I graduated with an Associates Degree in Gerontology.

I received an internship at a nursing home where I met many people. There I would spend time with the elderly outside on the patio where they would talk and smoke. After college, it was tough finding a job in gerontology because every nursing home or assisted living community I applied to wanted employees to lift people or catch them if they were about to fall. This was impossible for me due to my own disability. I am still interested in this type of career and hopeful someone will hire me to work with the elderly community.

CHAPTER SEVEN

My Walking Challenges

"Keep walking on straight paths, so that the lame foot may not be disabled, but instead be healed."

- *Hebrews 12:13*

When I was in my early twenties, my family and I went to Philadelphia to fix my toe drop problem and leg length discrepancy that was derived from my brain tumor. My toe drop problem affected my left foot which meant that these muscles were weak and I often stumbled. The orthopedic surgeon had to do a procedure on my ankle so that my toe wouldn't drag anymore; when I walked before the surgery I would stumble. The surgery lengthened the Achilles tendon which was too tight for my toe to come up. To this day, I still live with leg length discrepancy.

After my surgery, I walked a lot better and had physical therapy during which I did many stretches and exercises to strengthen my foot and leg. I feel ashamed to admit that I didn't practice the exercises at home as much as I should have. After I recovered from my surgery my parents battled with the insurance company to get a device called a walk-aide to help my toes go up when I walk. The walk-aide would give an electronically stimulated signal to my brain that would tell my shin muscle to pull my toe up. This device helped me walk better and corrected my tripping.

CHAPTER EIGHT

Restored Faith

"But after you have suffered for a little while,

the God of all grace, who calls you to share his

eternal glory in union with Christ, will himself

perfect you and give you firmness, strength, and a

sure foundation."

- *1 Peter 5:10*

My dad was a police officer, and his job had a strong impact on his life, including on his faith. He was always a believer and came from an immensely religious family, but he was questioning his faith throughout his entire life. While my dad was in the police department, he said he couldn't see the amount of love in the world because of all the pain he saw on a daily basis.

In my dads words, "Through the years of my life, I had gradually stopped praying. I had become accustomed to relying on my own wisdom and strength to get through daily problems. It wasn't until I had nowhere to turn, hit a brick wall, and was helpless that I came to a place where I turned to God. I wanted to turn to God, but I was afraid and didn't know how to talk to him. I called a priest whom I knew in Upstate New York and asked him to help me pray as I should. The priest said to him, "Carmine, just talk to God. Prayers are designed to help people communicate with God, but, all you have to do is spill your heart out. He hears you."

When I got sick, everything changed. When dad felt hopeless he turned to God. I was one of the reasons he regained his faith due to the miracle that happened to me at Medjugorje. I helped him to believe in God again.

Not having other people worry about me is something I desire. I want to give all that I can when I get back into volunteering. I have to work hard strengthening my legs, never giving into temptation to take the easy way out, and never losing my beliefs.

CHAPTER NINE

Community Support Systems

*God is not unfair. He will not forget the work
you did or the love you showed for him in the help
you gave and are still giving to your fellow
Christians.*
-     *Hebrews 6:10*

After years had passed, I started receiving assistance from a non-profit organization funded by the state of Maryland in my community. They provided me with life and job coaches. A life coach is responsible for helping individuals identify and accomplish their goals, while also integrating and interacting within their communities, whereas a job coach helps people find jobs, maintain current employment, create resumes, and prepare for interviews.

In the past, I only was able to have one life coach; however, now that my funding has changed, I can receive more help. My life coaches help me with activities such as cooking, cleaning, exercising, gardening and just hanging out. They help me to achieve my goals and think of new goals. They are tough but fair, and they remind me to drink my water.

My parents and I are a big part of the hiring process. The life coaches come to my house with my case manager so I can interview them. During this interview, I ask questions to help me get to know them better. Then, if everything goes well, I sign an agreement. So far, I am happy with the life coaches they have provided.

The organization allows me to participate in activities like dancing, painting and aerobics. My life coaches take me places like the movies, shopping, and accompany my mom or dad to my therapy when needed. I never had any best friends growing up, so I learned that my family and my life coaches are my true friends.

When I was twenty-seven I met one of the most important people in my life, Bettie, one of my life coaches and now a good friend of mine even though she hasn't worked for me in a few years. I met her through a mutual friend, Karen, who told Bettie about me and thought we would hit it off and so we did. Bettie tells me that her favorite part about meeting me was how quickly we connected. We bonded over how much we have in common and she appreciates my bubbly personality. We love cooking together, skiing, kayaking, dancing, karaoke nights, reading, bocce and many more activities.

I met Bettie's family for the first time after she got to know me better. She has four boys that are exceptionally sweet; Alex is the baby, then comes Maximus, Daniel and the oldest is Tommy. One of the things I remember about meeting Bettie is that her husband Mike and her four sons made me feel welcomed and no one made me feel like I was different. We still keep in touch and probably always will.

CHAPTER TEN

Unexpected & Unfortunate News

"He is not afraid of receiving bad news;

His faith is strong, and he trusts in the Lord."

-   *Psalm 112:7*

When I was twenty eight, in 2014, my parents took me on a trip to France. While in France, we stopped in Bordeaux where we toured a winery. We went down into the catacomb wine cellar to see all the barrels of wine that the winery produced. After being down there for a while, I began feeling lightheaded, so my parents were worried that something was wrong with me. I felt dizzy and knew that I had to get out of that place. Unfortunately, I did not feel any better even after I left. I feared that was a sign that something was wrong with me.

When we arrived back home my parents contacted the original surgeon at NYU and he referred us to a doctor in Maryland. After my MRI at Johns Hopkins, the neurosurgeon sat us down in his office and told us the news. I had another brain tumor. However, unlike the first one, this tumor was benign. It was attached to my skull and was likely caused by physical trauma or radiation, which made a whole lot of sense because I endured both when I was a small child.

When I was in remission for many years, the doctors felt I didn't need any more MRIs at that time. That might have been the reason why the tumor grew to the size of a golf ball. We did not expect the presence of another brain tumor since it had been twenty something years since my last one. I was a wreck, but my mom was unusually strong. She told me to trust in Jesus and pray, so I did. I felt overwhelmed, and I said to myself, "Why after all these years?" But with my faith in my God and determination as well as support from my family, I have been recovering. I feel thankful to God for always healing and keeping me in his protection. I am thankful to my family for never giving up on me.

I needed a neurosurgeon since the doctor recommended by New York only cared for children, so we were referred to a doctor named Dr. B. Mom was a little hesitant at first. She thought that he might not have as much experience with opening up a person for surgery due to how young he was. The doctor who was head of neurosurgery put my mother's mind at ease by saying that if he had a daughter he would have completely trusted Dr. B.. Although he is young, he is one of the best in his field. I believe that is when I felt mom finally relaxed. When we had the chance to meet this doctor, he was so nice, and he thoroughly answered every question we had. He said he wouldn't ever do anything that he did not think I could recover from. He also said that he would never do any procedure if he did not think that it was necessary.

CHAPTER ELEVEN

Undergoing Surgery and Recovery

"Lord heal me and I will be completely well;

rescue me and I will be perfectly safe. You

are the one I praise!"

- *Jeremiah 17:14*

In my case, the tumor was stuck to the meninges and skull and going into the brain. Because of the size of this tumor it was necessary to act immediately. Dr. B impressed my mom and dad by stating these facts, and he brought it all home when he said, "I have a daughter, and I would feel comfortable making the decision that was made here for her as well, if I had to." He went on to say, "If it would make you feel more comfortable, you can have me as the primary surgeon and the head of our department as your secondary doctor." That meant that Dr. B would perform my surgery, and I feel we made the best choice in my circumstance. My doctors and God helped me so much to overcome this obstacle in my life, all while guiding me through my journey of healing.

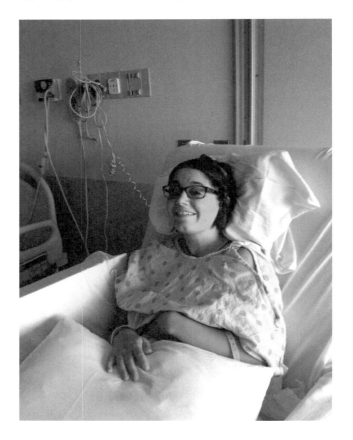

Dr. B removed most of the tumor and
burned the rest of the existing tumor. It had spread,
so if he had removed all of it, that would have

caused a stroke. I had a team of professionals helping me. After the operation, I could not move any part of my body from my neck down due to paralysis and spent the whole summer in the hospital. I gradually got back on my feet. With the help of my faith, family, therapy, friends, and determination, I slowly improved. My friend Bette, and my sister stayed with me some nights while I was in the hospital to give my parents a break.

Later, I started physical therapy again at Johns Hopkins, where I had to be re-evaluated by my therapists. They said I had made a lot of progress. Previously, when I walked, I couldn't have any distractions—even seemingly small things like saying hello to others. I recently overcame that challenge. I now can have brief conversations with people when I walk.

CHAPTER TWELVE

Baseline

"Friends always show their love,

What are brothers for if not to share trouble?"

-    *Proverbs 17:17*

I didn't talk to a lot of people in John Hopkins Hospital, but there I met another woman with a brain tumor. She was an older woman who had had a number of surgeries on her brain. When I heard that, I thought to myself, "Thank God I only had to go through a fraction of that."

I used to keep in contact with her and see her from time to time in therapy. She was a good friend when I was in the hospital who was there for me when I needed her, so I will never forget her generosity to me. At the time, I felt self-conscious because I was completely bald. She invited me to her room to play cards and hang out. We played the card game War, and we each won one round. Because we had the same experiences in the same hospital, we encouraged each other to get better, work hard, and never give up. I feel so thankful that our paths crossed. We became friends, and I feel so blessed to have known this woman. We gave encouragement and strength to each other—the best gift I could receive. I haven't seen her since I was discharged before her.

When the doctors sought to discharge me I still couldn't walk that well, so I asked the discharging doctor if I could stay another month to gain more of my mobility back. The discharging doctor's supervisor, who was the head of the department, decided it was a good idea. The goals I had for myself was to get back to my abilities that I had before like walking just with a gait (a limp). I had a great team working with me and gained mobility back slowly with the help of my parents and intense therapy. I was eventually almost back to my baseline.

CHAPTER THIRTEEN

A Setback

"I am the Lord your God;

I strengthen you and tell you,

'Do not be afraid; I will help you.' "

-    *Isaiah 41:13*

A couple of months later, after I had physical therapy, I was out with my life coach eating lunch, when she thought that there was food in my hair. When she took a closer look, She was perplexed, because instead what she saw was liquid running down my skull. She immediately took a photo of my head and sent it to my parents. I was taken home and my parents immediately took me back to Johns Hopkins to see what was wrong. My team of doctors explained that there was puss coming out of my skull and decided that it was best for me to have an MRI. The doctors discovered that I had an infection in my skull. This was a moment where I realized that I had a setback.

The best course of action was to go home

and take antibiotics to lessen the infection in my skull. The antibiotics were too strong to be inserted directly into my veins, therefore, the antibiotics were inserted through a PICC line that went straight to my heart. On a daily basis, for six months, I took medication through a PICC line and was immobile at home. I had to stay in bed and to be honest, I don't remember a lot of that time. I'm glad that I don't remember a lot because that experience was really traumatic for me. During this time, I had to wear a helmet because the doctors had to take out a part of my skull. I had no bone in the top section of my skull. After six months the infection decreased enough so I could have surgery. The doctors inserted man made material, made by a computer to fit exactly in the space where my bone was missing.

Following my surgery, I went to the intensive care unit and stayed in the hospital for a month to recover. When I came out, I had to wear a rubber helmet that had little holes (so my skin could breathe) to protect my brain and afterwards, I started to wear a headscarf. I also had to do outpatient therapy all over again.

Recovering from this tumor was a whole lot different than the last, because I began having seizures with this one following the infection. I had multiple seizures, including grand mal seizures, which are really scary and caused me to go unconscious. There were times when paramedics were called because the seizure was lasting too long. I also had physical convulsions during which my whole body shook. Thankfully, I haven't had a seizure in a long time. I'm crediting that to my diet, which helped me achieve this goal. The diet is called the Keto diet or the Ketogenic diet, and it's not just a diet, it's a medical treatment. One of my doctors said that people with epilepsy thrived with this treatment. The Ketogenic diet involves limiting carbohydrates and sugar intake, which is essential because my doctor told me, "Sugar feeds tumors." Until recently, grocery stores did not have a lot of Keto friendly foods for me, so my mother had to make everything from scratch. I am grateful for the variety of foods available to me now. This tumor has been a struggle, because I have to learn how to walk again as well as regain my balance and strength through hip and leg exercises.

CHAPTER FOURTEEN

Therapy

"Don't you know that your body is a temple of the

Holy Spirit, who lives in you and who was given

to you by God?"

-    *1 Corinthians 6:19-20*

I do many different types of therapy, such as horseback riding therapy, which engages my abs through turning as well as balancing on the saddle while I listen to the instructor in the arena. For example, she gives me directions to follow so that I can guide the horse and complete tasks in the form of games. I also do tap therapy where my muscles get tapped to stimulate them in an effort to retrain my brain. My therapist said that the brain is blind, so it needs help seeing the muscles that need to be activated again. This type of therapy I receive involves a neurodevelopmental treatment technique called tapping, or proprioceptive neuromuscular facilitation, as well as massage therapy, which relaxes my muscles and relieves stress.

When I walk in therapy, I am still using my

walker, but now I am practicing walking without it as well. I'm still working on therapy at home, as well, which has been a struggle without my therapists from Johns Hopkins around because my parents and my support staff don't have the necessary experience or training. I also balance on my knees which helps my muscles, my stomach, legs and glute muscles. My physical therapist gives me and my support team exercises to follow at home to encourage my recovery. My support team at Johns Hopkins is always very pleased with my progress. Now I just have to get my confidence back so I can walk with rhythm. And I will!

Not all of my therapists have been so supportive, though. I had a lot of therapists who said not to continue therapy after I progressed to a certain point, or when I hit what they consider a "peak" by their standards. By this, they meant I wouldn't make any more progress. Their doubt in my exceeding expectations made me feel depressed. However, with God's help I prevailed, and I am still having miracles every day. I believe that someday I will walk again without any assistance. In the meantime, I will use only a cane. I keep making progress so I won't need walking aids or my life coaches anymore. I don't want anyone getting the wrong opinion that I am not grateful for my services, because I definitely am. It's just that I ultimately want to be independent like everyone else.

CHAPTER FIFTEEN

Reflection

"Children are a gift from the Lord;

They are a real blessing."

- *Psalm 127:3*

In 2017, we moved from our house due to problems I was having getting around including being able to get up and down the stairs safely. We found property across the road from my brother and his family. A beautiful house was built for my needs. It's a one level home, with a small apartment attached. I love my apartment, with my own space, which has a kitchen, living room, bedroom and a large bathroom. My apartment is attached to my parents' living space. I am surrounded by farmland along with beautiful scenery. I love seeing all the wildlife and hearing the cows mooing. I also love the fact that I am near my brother, his wife and my nephews. I see them practically every day. Also, I am blessed that my sister lives a short distance away and I get to see her family, including my two nieces and nephew several times a week. I am grateful to my parents for going the extra mile to help me through every step of my life. If I can give one piece of advice to my readers it is to respect your parents. Love them, they are another gift from God who loved us first, then He gave us our parents.

I had another unexpected opportunity to travel to Medjugorje in August of 2021. Again in 2020 my family faced another crisis. My sister who was pregnant with her second child was told after she had her first sonogram that her child had severe medical issues and she would not likely survive. She was advised many times by the medical staff to abort the child. During the entire pregnancy we prayed constantly for this child. Her daughter was born with and by the grace of God many of the serious medical conditions resolved themselves after her birth. The only condition that is still outstanding is a small hole in the upper ventricle of her heart that may very well close on its own. Therefore, we decided to go back as a family on a pilgrimage to thank The Blessed Mother for interceding to God on our behalf.

When we arrived in Medjugorje a yearly youth festival was taking place. There were tens of thousands of young people and thousands of priests from all over the world. I can't even explain what a feeling it was seeing so many young people singing and praising God. Being there was remarkable in so many ways, especially sharing it with my sister, brother- in-law, nieces and my brother in law's mother who also accompanied us and in fact planned this trip. Although most of the people were ones we had never met before, there was a feeling we had known them all our lives. The love and caring I felt was surreal.

One evening after mass we met a priest outside Saint James Church and asked him if they were having a healing mass later that night. He didn't know but he immediately put his belongings down on the ground and placed his hands on my head and started to pray a prayer of healing. Another event occurred when we were walking in town after mass and a couple stopped to pray with us. That same evening, we took a taxi to return back to the house where we were staying. Also, I want to mention, every taxi we took had a religious article displayed in their car. When we arrived at our destination my father went to pay the driver but he wouldn't take any payment. My father kept insisting but the driver who didn't speak English wouldn't take the money. He took off with a quick handshake and a hug. Could you imagine if every small town were like this town of Medjugorje? Prayer, love and respect for God, brings peace, love and respect for one another and life.

Although on this trip, my father was not able to help me up the mountain, I was still able to go even though I still can't walk. Five young men volunteered to carry me up in a specially designed chair. If you can picture the way Cleopatra was transported, with two men in the front and two in the back with a seat in the middle, you will have a good idea of what I looked like. I felt so blessed to be able to get to the top of Cross Mountain and pray in front of the statue of Our Blessed Mother and where Our Lady first appeared to the children.

Much has changed in Medjugorje since my last visit. Streets and paved roads now exist where there was once only dirt roads. Restaurants, stores and hotels now line the streets in the town. Although, even with all the changes, Medjugorje still feels like heaven on earth. God's presence and the love of Mother Mary is felt the moment you arrive.

My family is the main reason that I am writing this autobiography. I know they already know that I appreciate them, but I just want to remind them that I see their love and efforts through all of the hard patches we went through in my life.

I have learned in my life that you do not need a lot of friends, you just need the love and the support of family around you. I used to think that I wanted the same childhood experience as my sister. My little sister Mary-Christine used to have sleepovers, and she used to go out with her friends. They treated me as a friend, too, but it still wasn't the same. I know that I still have friends because I have God, my family, my life coaches and the friends I talk to on the phone. I am so blessed. The question everyone should ask themselves is, "Are you surrounded by people who love you?" If so, then those people are true friends. My family are my true friends. I am extremely grateful and thank

God, for everyone in my life: my parents, sisters, brothers, nieces and nephews. They give me a purpose in my everyday life.

Through the years of my life I, along with my family, attended countless healing services. There was one man in particular, Father Dennis Kelleher who had a healing ministry. We followed him as he took his congregation on religious retreats to Saint Anne's in Quebec, Canada and other religious sites in Canada and the upper New York area. We also went with him to Europe. We visited the holy sites where Mother Mary appeared, in Lourdes, France, and Fatima, Portugal. There were so many other churches we visited while in Europe. Father Dennis knew my father was the only one working in the family and couldn't afford these trips but somehow he always made them affordable to my parents. Father Dennis embraced me from the onset of my illness at two years old and his staff and prayer group were continually praying for me. To know him was to feel the presence of Christ and a deep penetrating love. Before starting mass we would always say the rosary and after the rosary he would hold up his Bible and say, "What does the word BIBLE mean; B is for basic, I is for information, B is before, L is for Leaving, E is for Earth. **B**asic **I**nformation **B**efore **L**eaving **E**arth." He impressed upon us how important it was to read the Bible. I remember speaking to him when he was no longer able to celebrate masses due to his illness, that he was still concerned about me and asked how I was doing. These memories enable me to remain positive and deeply connected to my faith and knowing all of humanity is in need of God. Father Kellher passed away on February 20, 2002. I still miss him so much.

Boy, growing up with a disability during the '90s was not easy to say the least, but I survived. I feel I am a lot stronger because I faced my disabilities head on without complaining. My life has been blessed because of faith, family and friends who have always been there for me when I've needed them. Faith is the main reason I can overcome the things I had to endure and will continue to overcome. No one knows as much as I do what it's like to be me. I want more of the simplest things such as walking by myself, going to the restroom and showering independently, going on dates, preparing meals, working outside of

home. I want to be what everyone wants to be:

successful. I don't want to be the one who falls

through the cracks like lots of other people living

with disabilities. To be viewed as an individual and

not defined by my disability is the dream that every

person like me has. I want to get back to being

involved with the Special Olympics. I knew from

the beginning that I would have to work hard. I had

a skilled group of therapists working with me. They

loved that I was so determined to get better. They

always said that I was one of the most dedicated

patients that they had ever seen.

CHAPTER SIXTEEN

My Ongoing Miracles

"It was because you do not have

enough faith," answered Jesus,

"I assure you that if you have faith

as big as a mustard seed, you can say to

this hill, 'Go from here to there!' and it

will go. You could do anything!"

-       *Matthew 17:20*

I wouldn't be here without God, Mother Mary and my family. They are the reason I am here today writing my experiences down. I am grateful to have others read my story and to inspire people who are going through trials in their lives. I want everyone to know there is always a way to persevere. You can pray to God to heal you. Sometimes he allows us to experience pain in order to fulfill a bigger purpose in life. I try to pray to the rosary every night to maintain a connection with God, Our Creator. We need to pray for one another so as to strengthen our faith, as well as to reach out to one another, because we all need love and respect. I wouldn't be here without prayer and the power of God and the prayers of Mother Mary as well as the love and support from the countless people known and unknown to me.

THE END

OUR LADY OF MEDUGORJE

This is a drawing of Mary as The Visionaries have seen her when she appeared to them.

~

Mother Mary's Message from March 14, 1985

"Dear children! In your life, you have all experienced light and darkness. God lets every person recognise good and evil. I am calling you to the light which you should carry to all the people who are in darkness. Daily, people who are in darkness come into your homes. Dear children, give them the light! Thank you for having responded to my call."

My Most Recent Trip to Medjugorje in

September 2023

This is the last stop on Apparition Hill where

people pray to Our Lady. You see me with one of the

men praying.

This is me in front of The Weeping Cross.

Picture of me getting ready to go up Apparition

Hill.

Praying to Mother Mary with my parents.

A Rose From Heaven

Made in the USA
Columbia, SC
20 March 2024

33355722R00067